LESSONS TO LIVE BY:
THE CANINE
COMMANDMENTS

LESSONS TO LIVE BY: THE CANINE COMMANDMENTS

*The Commandments of Life,
As Dogs Would Write Them*

by

W.R. Pursche

Revised Second Edition

The author is grateful to the publisher for permission to reprint excerpts from
the following:

Roy Blout poems, from IF ONLY YOU KNEW HOW MUCH I SMELL
YOU by Roy Blout. Copyright © 1998 by Roy Blout (Text); Copyright © 1998
by Valerie Shaff (Photographs). By permission of Little, Brown and Company,
(Inc.)

Cover photograph by Kim Windsor.

10 9 8 7 6 5

ISBN: 0-975379-348

Published in the United States by Varzara House.

Contents

Everyone thinks that their dog is the best dog in the world.
And none of them are wrong.

Preface to the Second Edition

It has been over ten years since I wrote the principal elements of *Lessons to Live By: The Canine Commandments,* and now more than three years have passed since the first edition of the book. During that time I have received hundreds of emails and messages from readers and from others who have heard about the lessons, or who have wanted to offer examples of new lessons, or who have stories about how they have learned from their dogs. In a number of cases I have even received as suggestions some of the lessons that are already in the book, perhaps passed from person to person over the anonymous magic of the Internet, their original context lost. Seeing some of my own words sent back to me (sometimes with stories attached) is heartwarming. Such is the appeal of the lessons, and lends credence to the premise that the examples set by our canine companions are so powerful that they shout out to us even across the divide of our species.

Many have asked how these lessons have changed my life, and about whether the dogs mentioned in the original story ("After") are real. So this Second Edition includes a new story ("Before") that answers, at least in part, some of those questions.

So that we will all have as many dogs as possible to help guide us and give us examples of these and many other lessons, 100% of the net proceeds of this edition will be dedicated to the saving and care of dogs (and some other animals too).

W.R. Pursche
January, 2003

Acknowledgements

To my Mom and Dad, for always being supportive in whatever I have wanted to do; to Mark DiLuglio and Mike Gabriele, for all the confidence and help through the years; to W.T. "Wink" Mason, dog handler *extraordaire*, for all the patience and for teaching me how to be a handler; to Dennis Tracz, for his lesson on 'net positives'; to Kira Higgs, for her insights into spirituality and self expression; to Mr. Walt Jagger, for picking out the perfect pup for me, to Christy Parsons, for the inspiration, and especially to Kim Silhanek, for all her help and support, and most of all for coming with me on that long car ride that September.

And to Roy, who is so smart that he probably made some improvements to these lessons when I wasn't looking. In one way or another he is responsible for much of what comes next.

The most curious part of the thing was, that the trees and other things round them never changed their places at all: however fast they went, they never seemed to pass anything. "I wonder if all the things move along with us?" thought poor puzzled Alice. And the Queen seemed to guess her thoughts, for she cried "Faster! Don't try to talk!"

...And they went so fast that at last they seemed to skim through the air, hardly touching the ground with their feet, till suddenly, just as Alice was getting quite exhausted, they stopped...

...Alice looked around her in great surprise. "Why, I do believe we've been under this tree the whole time! Everything's just as it was!"

"Of course it is," said the Queen. "What would you have it?"

"Well, in our country," said Alice, still panting a little, "you'd generally get to get somewhere else – if you ran very fast for a long time, as we've been doing."

"A slow sort of country! said the Queen. "Now, here, you see, it takes all the running you can do, to keep in the same place. If you want to get somewhere else, you must run at least twice as fast as that!"

— Lewis Carroll, *Through the Looking Glass*

Before

Not so very long ago, at an enviously early age, I had achieved more than I had ever expected in life. I had just left a great organization with which I had had a rich and enjoyable career to start my own company, I had a great new house, and had made more money than I had ever dreamed I would make. On top of this, through no work on my part, I was blessed with great parents, supportive and loyal friends, and good health.

Yet, while I cannot say that I was unhappy, I seemed to be on a treadmill. Life just swept by me, and I always felt that I needed to do just one more thing, and then I'd be able to really 'start doing what I wanted to in life.' Usually the 'one thing' took months or even years, and of course at the end (or often along the way) a whole new set of 'one things to do' came along.

In my case, what I wanted to do was not a specific activity or goal, but rather I wanted to have a life where I was not so driven (and defined) by what I did and what job I had. Like most people, I saw life as what you fit in when you weren't working or doing other things. I too thought that it made sense to think of 'balancing' work and life.

But I didn't want to 'balance' anything, because to me balance always implied too many tradeoffs, and the feeling that whenever I was doing one thing (like working) I was missing something else (life) and vice versa. Instead, what I really wanted, when I had time to think about it, was the other way around — I wanted my work, what I did for a living, to be *integrated* into my life. I just wanted to feel that my life would be a single process that would be made up of a combination of experiences and activities; some would be work and others would not be. But I almost didn't have time to figure out how to do this, because, like everyone else, I was *too busy.*

One day, on one of my rare breaks from work, travel, and 'stuff ' I had to do, I attended a sheepdog competition not far from where I live. I don't know if you have ever been to a sheepdog competition or have seen one on TV (if not, I suggest you try to!) but this is where dogs, usually border collies, compete to herd sheep. A big field is set up, with gates and pens, and a dog and his handler go out in the field, and working as a team, they have to gather up the sheep and move them across the field in a predetermined way, and put them in a pen. It is a casually festive affair. Unlike the people you find at formal dog shows, most sheepdog people are farmers, and the entire activity, while very serious for the participants, seems much more relaxed and fun. Certainly the dogs think it is fun. If you don't believe that it's possible to be 100 percent serious while having fun, then you haven't seen a border collie work sheep.

Now, at this event, there were hundreds of dogs. Many were competing, but others were just there because their owners were. Some handlers travel a thousand miles to go to a big trial, and of course they travel with their dogs.

So picture a big field, where the competition is being held, and behind it another field, filled with trucks and campers, where all the handlers are staying for a few days. Some of the handlers may have five or more dogs with them. While they are not competing, the dogs are usually kept in their crates (which they like because it is 'home' to them), or tied near their trailers, where they can sit in the shade.

I had been to a few trials, and always found it fun not only to watch the trial but also to. walk around the area where all the dogs were waiting. I had met quite a few nice people this way, and a lot of great dogs (most of the handlers are happy to let you visit with their dogs, but of course it's good to ask first).

I came upon one trailer with Pennsylvania plates that had two dogs tied near it. They seemed especially friendly, wagging their tails and getting a little excited as I came near, and I could tell they really wanted a pat. I looked around for their owner, but there was no one at the trailer. I figured that the handler must have been off watching the trial. I walked around the field some more, and when I came back about a half hour later, these two dogs were still there, and just as excited to see me. The owner still had not returned. This isn't so surprising –

"working" dogs are often so well behaved that they don't run off even if not tied, and they usually work so hard that their handlers sometimes leave them alone when they are not working so that they can rest.

Well, it was pretty obvious that these two wanted to be pet, so I offered up my hand, and soon thereafter I had made two friends. These were two of the most congenial border collies that I had ever met. (Border collies, while often friendly, are usually mostly interested in working and their handlers – often in that order).

I was a little bit depressed due to my hectic life at that time, and I really needed a good pat too. It was as if these dogs understood how I felt and were saying "Be happy! Life is good!"

I stayed there for long time, but then sadly I had to go, and did not get to meet their owner.

A whole year went by. I never could have imagined how, but the year was busier than ever before. I was traveling constantly, working a lot of hours, and ever on the go. It's not that things were not going well, in fact, everything was as it was before, just more so.

One day a friend called to let me know that a sheepdog trial was coming up. It turned out to be the same trial that I had attended the year before. Half jokingly I said, "I met these two great dogs there last year. I bet if I go, they'll be there again, and they'll remember me."

Well, I did go, and the same two dogs were there, and I swear they remembered me. I'm sure it was that they were just friendly dogs, but at the time it really seemed that they remembered who I was, and it was a nice feeling.

Once again I looked around for their owner, to no avail. On the way out (although it was a Sunday, I was leaving to catch a plane to travel for work, which is how my life was going), I stopped to watch one more run. An older woman was the handler, and it was great to watch the way she and her dog worked together. Handlers and their dogs have a special bond, and you can feel it at a trial.

After the run, when she came off the field, I congratulated her and asked her some question; I forget what it was. She answered, and then asked me if I had a dog. I said no, almost apologetically. (I mean, I couldn't very well have a dog, with my work and my travel and all my responsibilities, could I?)

I told her that I when I was young I had grown up with a great dog named Sam. Our family had got him when he was a pup and I was 7, and he died when I was 28. Although by that time I was 'grown up' and away working in the big city, you can imagine how much a part of my life he had been. But I had not had a dog in a long time, now that I was *so busy*.

I also told her that I loved going to trials. She then told me that there was going to be another trial the following week, much smaller and more intimate, on her farm, which was not far away, and that I should go.

A week later I was there, and she was right, it was a much smaller affair. You could watch from behind a low fence that was very close to where the dogs were working, and it was amazing to see how hard they worked while still seeming to really enjoy what they were doing.

I went walking through the field where all the dogs and trailers were, and you won't believe it — but I came across the same two dogs! (I later learned that this was not surprising, because once the trial season starts, some handlers just go from trial to trial.) But at the time I thought that I was fated to constantly see these dogs. Once again I was convinced they remembered me, and once again they really cheered me up.

This time, I resolved not to leave until I met their owner. And sure enough, he was there in the trailer. He was an older gentleman, very quiet and calm. It turns out he had been training and trialing dogs for decades. Later I watched him in a trial and unlike many of the other handlers, he gave very few commands to his dogs. He just seemed to understand the 'flow' of their work, and was able to be part of it without having to constantly interject himself into the process. It was like Zen dog handling, if you can imagine that.

We talked for a bit, and I got his name and the name of the two dogs: Roy and Celt. I went home, happy to finally know about them.

Months later, I had a very difficult travel and work week, capping off a stretch of time that I'm sure you've experienced, where every little thing seems to go wrong – like missing planes, getting stuck in traffic, the car breaking down – all at the 'worst time.' Everything was giving me the feeling that I was in a giant battle with life, and I was losing.

After one especially tough day, I wrote a letter to the owner of those two dogs. I still don't really know what possessed me to do it, except that I had this nagging feeling that I needed some change in my life, and that dogs would be part of that change. In the letter, I reminded him of our meeting — and here is the crazy part — I asked him if either one of the two dogs I had met ever fathered pups, whether I could get one. Now I say this was "crazy" because I felt there was simply no way that I could have a dog. I was traveling three days a week and working really hard, and still constantly felt that I was falling farther behind. There was no room in my life for anything new, let alone a dog.

A few more months went by and I didn't think too much about it, but one night the phone rang, and it was the man to whom I had written. He apologized for not calling sooner, but it turns out that he had been very ill, and had been in and out of the hospital for treatments. He said this matter of factly, and I felt embarrassed for thinking that my life was tough! He referred to my letter and said that he really didn't breed dogs much anymore, but since he had over 20 dogs on his farm, every so often there would in fact be a litter (some planned, some not). Unfortunately, all his pups were "spoken for" for the next two years. (I later learned that all his dogs had the same amazing temperament as Roy and Celt, and this is one of the reasons that they are is such high demand. I also concluded that this was not simply a result of breeding but a reflection of their owner). And while he would be happy to put me on the waiting list for a pup, he didn't want to promise me anything and have me be disappointed, since – as he put it – he might not "be around" in two years.

I didn't know what to say. Here was someone who was quite sick and who was worried about whether I'd be disappointed about not getting a dog. I kind of mumbled something like "I'm sure you'll be fine," said I would of course wait as long as it took, and we hung up.

I didn't see or speak to him for a long time, but from some other handlers that I spoke with I did hear that he was progressing with his treatments.

Then late on one Friday night, during a terrible rain that had lasted three days and had disrupted my travel plans so much that I was having to work extra hours again, the phone rang. It was him. He is not a man of many words, and he said simply "Well, I'm still here. You are still on the waiting list, but it will probably be another six months before you'd get a pup. But I do have a pup here that is about 8 weeks old. The man that he was promised to could not take him at the last minute. He is Celt's grandson – Celt is too old to have his own pups now. I remembered that you wanted a pup from Celt or Roy. This wasn't a planned litter, and to tell you the truth I'm not sure how good of a working dog he will be, but he's one of the best looking pups I've ever seen, and he has a nice disposition. If you want to see him I can hold him for you for the weekend."

So suddenly I was at a point that I had not really planned for. It had been easy before to express interest in getting a dog, especially after finding out that it took so long. There had been no immediate need to make a decision, or to face the reality of the situation. But here it was, not only very immediate, but with a deadline.

I felt that I had to go at least see the pup, given that he was making this nice offer. I was so far behind at work anyway that not working the weekend wasn't going to make matters any worse than they already were.

I called a friend and asked her half seriously if she would be willing to go see the pup with me, and that it would be a nine hour drive in the rain. She agreed anyway, and if she had not I might not have gone, such was my indecision.

The next day we set out, making our way north the hundreds of miles through the hard rain. At one point one of my windshield wipers broke (the one on the driver's side, of course) and I had to fix it in a parking lot, getting soaked in the process. What in the world was I doing here? While I was fiddling with the repair, and later, on the long drive, I kept telling myself that I was probably wasting my time – no matter how nice the dog, *now* just wasn't the right time for this.

Of course, in the back of my mind I did have some thoughts of what life might be like with a dog. I had even decided that since this pup had Celt's genes, I could name the pup Roy, after the other dog. But I really couldn't see it happening, and I would have to be content with a dream of a world with a dog named Roy in it.

By the time we reached the farm the sun had come out. The day had turned so crisp and clear that the cold rain of the day and night before was nothing but a memory that was hard to retrieve. The man that I had come to see was waiting for me, and he took me into a small barn. In the barn was a series of stalls arrayed along each wall, like horse stalls, only smaller. In each stall there was a dog, and as you walked down the center aisle all the dogs could see you coming. I went from stall to stall and all the dogs were like Roy and Celt, friendly and happy to see me (and especially their owner, whom they clearly loved. Someone later once said, "I'd die a happy person if just once a dog would look at me the way all his dogs look at him.") Roy and Celt were there too, and having met them a few times now I was sure that they in fact did remember me.

In the last stall there was one female dog that was clearly a mother, and one pup following her around in the straw. The pup stopped as soon as he heard us, and immediately tried to get close, reaching up as high as he could, trying to balance on his small legs.

I had not been misled. This *was* the best looking pup in the world. The man picked him up and put him in my arms, and from that instant my life would never be the same.

* * *

Many a time I have been aware that my dogs have been trying to tell me something. But I am unable to cross the frontier into the dog's mind. They, it seems to me, can cross the frontier into mine whenever they wish. The fact is that the dog can live, happily and at ease, in two worlds: his and our own.

— Brian Vesey-Fizgerald, *Animal Anthology*

A Dog's Life

Have you ever thought about trading places with a dog? Just for a minute? Or even living a dog's life? Many people have. When we see dogs lying in the sun in a deep contented sleep, rolling in the grass, lifting their heads to a twilight breeze, we think: Wouldn't it be great to be a dog? Unlike us, dogs seem to have no worries; they seem to really enjoy living and get the most out of everything that they do. Most dogs just seem, well, happy all the time.

Yet if given the chance, of course, few people would actually trade places with a dog. And so this remains just another passing thought.

But what if we could take all that really does seem to be great about 'a dog's life' and integrate it into our human lives? Not trade places with a dog, but take all the things that make us envy dogs sometimes. Wouldn't that be the best of both worlds? Wouldn't then we really have the reality of 'a dog's life'?

Edward Hoagland said "In order to really enjoy a dog, one doesn't merely try to train him to be semihuman. The point of it is to open oneself to the possibility of becoming partly a dog." If you read any of today's self help books, or even some of the great philosophers, they are often telling us to behave and think much like dogs do. Well, they never come right out and say this of course, but when you get behind all of the advice, isn't that what a lot of it is all about? "Carpe Diem!" is one often-repeated theme – "Seize the day!" And who could argue with this advice – the idea of living every day to its fullest. Why should this be such a surprise to us? Isn't this exactly what we see dogs do every day? Each morning they wake up, and from the very first minute seem to put all their energy into *today*, not yesterday, not tomorrow. They don't seem to waste a minute, and yet aren't fretting about having too much to do, or being 'too busy.' If you really want to understand 'Seize the day' – just watch a dog!

Even if you don't have your own dog, you can still see much of what makes 'a dog's life' just by watching other people's dogs. Go to a park, and just watch. And talk to the people with the dogs – dogs are a great excuse to start a conversation with someone you don't know. What a way to make two friends at the same time! And while many people with children will start telling you stories about their kids with no prompting, people with dogs usually wait to be asked, but have the same depth of interesting stories. Even when people who are not 'dog lover's' or 'dog people' get introduced to dogs and get to spend time with them, they are often amazed at how interesting dogs are, and how they all have unique personalities. All dogs are dogs, of course, but each dog is not like every other dog. They are as individual as people are.

We can learn from both their simplicity and their uniqueness. Let's see what it means to live a dog's life.

* * *

Carlo died –

E. Dickinson

Would you instruct me now?

— from a letter written by
Emily Dickinson to a friend
after the death of her dog

The Canine Commandments

Why do we love dogs? While there are as many reasons as there are people (and dogs), the best explanation may be that we love dogs because they embody what many people strive for in life. Of course no one actually says it this way, but when you come to think of it, if you were to ask people what they think of as 'good,' or 'how they should live life,' and then compared that list to how dogs live and act, you would see an amazing overlap. Emily Dickinson saw this, and her letter to someone she really respected seems to be saying "I was getting all my instruction from my dog Carlo, and now I need to get it elsewhere."

If dogs could write, and had a written history as we do, they might have at one point in time summarized their 'code of life' just as we have in our own Ten Commandments. Their code might look something like this:

1. Accept others for who they are and love them unconditionally.
2. Be loyal.
3. No matter what happens, or how much someone is mad at you, run back and make friends.
4. Be happy with who you are.
5. Live for today.
6. Go with the flow.
7. Life is the journey itself.
8. Make the world a better place.
9. Have fun!
10. Have everlasting and absolute faith.

Unlike our Ten Commandments, which mostly say "Don't do this" and "Don't do that" the Canine Commandments are all positive. Isn't it interesting that when we hear some positive guidance ("Do") it sounds like a vague platitude, but when expressed as a negative ("Don't") then we are more likely to listen? If someone says "Live life to its fullest!" or "Seize the day!" we are likely to roll our eyes, or say we agree but not really do anything differently, and yet when someone says "Don't waste time" we are more likely to try to change our behavior.

Of course, we could translate the Canine Commandments into negatives, like "Never pretend to be someone you are not" and "Don't hold grudges," but for some reason that doesn't feel like how dogs live and act. Dogs would never need to write down their "rules" either, even if they could, because their Commandments are part of them – it is what makes them, well, dogs.

Since we now have a list, let's explore these Commandments, and see what we can learn about dogs and about ourselves.

* * *

You can easily judge the character of a man by how he treats those who can do nothing for him or to him.

— Thomas Edison

I

Accept others for who they are and love them unconditionally

Have you ever seen how a dog acts when he meets a handicapped person? Notice anything different in how the dog reacts to the person? I'll bet you didn't. Because there is no difference in how a dog treats a person – whether the person be handicapped, or blind, or tall or short or black or white. To a dog, a new person is just another chance to meet a friend, or to have fun. But if you watch a person – maybe even yourself as they meet someone "different," you are likely to see them tense up, or get embarrassed, or otherwise not act themselves.

Dogs however, always seem to accept things – and people – for what they are. This is why dogs are brought to hospitals to visit sick people and cheer them up, because they treat everyone the same. They don't look away, or whisper, or avoid people who are sick. They are just themselves, and it works.

Unlike us, dogs also don't spend a lot of time trying to change other people into something else – or change themselves into something else.

> *Huitse said to Changtse, "I have a tree, and though it is large its trunk is so irregular and gnarled and its branches so twisted that it cannot be used for lumber. It stands right by the roadside, yet no carpenter will look at it. Your words are like that tree, big and useless, and no one pays attention to them.*
>
> *Changtse replied: Have you never seen a wild cat, crouching down in wait for its prey? It is always ready to pounce, right, left, high or low. But if it is too focused on its prey it can easily be captured, or fall into a net. On the other hand, there is the yak with its great big body. But for all its size it cannot catch mice. Now you have a large tree but fret over its uselessness. But even if it grew in the middle of nowhere, you could rest beneath it, and take advantage of its shade. Since it would be safe from any axe, nothing will harm it. It is useless to you only because you want to make it into something it is not."*
>
> —from *The Chuang-tzu*

The next time you are with a group of people, stop to listen to their conversation, and count how often the 'conversation' is really nothing more than people telling other people how they should behave or act. "Don't do that!" "Put some catsup on it, it will taste better." "Put on a sweater, it's cold." "Change the station." Sometimes what passes for conversation is nothing more than a subtle – or not so subtle – series of comments that in effect are people trying to get each other to change – to do what they want, to be like *them*. Oh, of course they sound like they are giving helpful advice, but really aren't they simply saying that "you" should be more like "me"? (Not that everyone is this way, of course, but it is sadly common). Like the story of the 'useless' tree, people often try to make those around them into someone they are not.

But even if they could talk, I doubt you'd hear dogs say, "Chew the stick this way!" Or "You should get your hair cut like mine!" Or "Too bad you are not a Golden Retriever" Or "Don't pet me, you only have two legs!" They wouldn't spend all their time telling other dogs – or people – what to do, how to do it, or how to live.

Dogs just accept others for what they are, and love them as they are.

* * *

But of thee it shall be said,
This dog watched beside a bed
Day and night unweary, —
Watched within a curtained room,
Where no sunbeam brake the gloom
Round the sick and dreary.

Roses, gathered for a vase,
In that chamber died apace,
Beam in breeze resigning;
This dog only, waited on,
Knowing that when light is gone
Love remains for shining.

— Elizabeth Barrett Browning, *To Flush, My Dog*

II

Be loyal

A dog's loyalty is so strong that it is often difficult to tell it apart from love, and faith in his companions, whether they be other dogs or people. There are entire books written about dogs being so loyal that they undertake remarkable journeys just to find their way home after being separated from a loved one.

Unlike people, dogs don't hold grudges, or easily give up their friendship and loyalty. Have you ever had a conversation with someone you had not seen in a while, and asked them about someone you knew they were close friends with? "Oh, I don't like Mary anymore," they say. "Why you always were such close friends!" "Well, she . . . " and what follows is supposed to explain what caused the loss of friendship. It might be something like a slight ("She was not nice to my new boyfriend!"), or a drifting off ("I was too busy"), or something else that, in the great scheme of things, seems really minor. It feels minor, of course, because it *is* minor.

To a dog, though, loyalty is constant and long-lasting:

> *I've met this wonderful dog, in Grace. He's half coyote and he'll sit for five hours in the back of a pickup truck waiting for you, just because he trusts you to come back.*
>
> — Barbara Kingsolver, *Animal Dreams*

'Loyalty,' of course, is just another way of saying 'trust' — in someone else, and in ourselves, to trust ourselves to choose the people to be loyal to. We don't need to do what dogs do — they often get no choice as to who they are loyal to, but we do. But once we make this choice — and we should — we can learn a lot from dogs, and trust in our choice.

Trust goes hand in hand with accepting the people in our lives for what they are. By trusting them, we can avoid the frustrations one often feels when someone won't do something exactly as you would have done it. You'd never see a dog stop playing with another dog because the other dog wanted to chew a different stick, or lie down instead of sit. And yet we do this all the time. We give our friends "helpful advice," and then get frustrated or even angry when they don't do what we suggested – often so frustrated that we lose all sense of perspective, and perhaps even turn our backs on them, or feel the need to say "I told you so!"

Dogs seem to keep it very simple, and seem to be saying to other dogs: "If you are good to me, then I'll be good to you.

Stand by me, and I'll do the same for you." Perhaps they can do this because they keep life simple, and are not confused by too much thought and worry.

Dogs can't pick up the phone and call an old friend, perhaps someone we have been too busy for, or someone who once slighted us, or someone that we never thanked for the many things they have done for us.

But we can.

Look not at the fault of others,
At what they have done or left undone;
Rather, look at what you yourself
Have done or left undone.

— Verse 50, from *The Dhammapada*

III

**No matter what happens, or how much
someone is mad at you, run back
and make friends**

To a dog, forgiveness may be one more element of loyalty.
To us it's probably a totally different thing, but the two go
hand in hand. Just as loyalty doesn't simply mean blindly
accepting and following someone else, forgiveness is
something we should think about and make a decision
about, but we should err on the side of being more
forgiving, especially when someone has made a simple
mistake, or has merely done something to slight us.

By first accepting people for who they are, and being loyal
(to them, and ourselves) we can easily accept that good people
can make mistakes, and well, be human.

In his book "Dogs Never Lie About Love," Jeffrey
Moussaieff Masson quotes this story from an old book:

A young man took a dog into a boat, rowed to the center of the Seine, and threw the animal over, with intent to drown him. The poor dog often tried to climb up the side of the boat; his master as often pushed him back, till, overbalancing himself, he fell overboard. As soon as the faithful dog saw his master in the stream, he left the boat and held him above water till help arrived from the shore, and his life was saved.

I doubt any of us can really ever be so forgiving, but dogs do this all the time. They forgive the transgressions of other dogs and of people. Have you ever seen two dogs get in a bit of a fight over something? One quick growl and it's over – no grudges, no hard feelings. The dogs just go on as if nothing happened.

We, on the other hand, hold all kinds of grudges. We have a hard time 'forgiving and forgetting.' Certainly if someone does something terribly bad to us, it probably is a good idea not to forget this, because in the end we need to protect our own selves (and self worth). And maybe such people should no longer be part of our lives. But the little slights (which in some cases are really no more than our own misunderstandings or insecurities) shouldn't linger. Some people seem to actually tally them all up, and store them in a big 'grudge book,' recalling them time and time again, and usually using them to try to do their own hurting. "I'm still mad at you for not spending more time with me last week." "Remember when you forgot my birthday?" All these and other little things constantly get stored away, simmering just below the surface, and poisoning our loves and friendships.

Dogs just don't do this. What's past is past. If it was so bad, then, for the sake of self-preservation, the dog will have nothing more to do with that dog or person. But for everything else, whether it be from another dog (the stolen bone, the too-hard bite during play) or from a person (the missed meal, the foot stepped on), there is immediate and absolute forgiveness. In her book *The Eternal Spiral of Life*, Birgit Klein writes about the forgiveness of dogs: "There is no pettiness and fussiness in any respect – always starting afresh and seeing each other in the shining light of the moment."

Dogs seem to understand what we don't: that we should surround ourselves with people that are a 'net positive' in our lives – people who bring us (and to whom we can bring), on the whole, more happiness, more fun, more learning, more love. In short, those who make us better people. For such people, we need to be more accepting and more forgiving, and there is no excuse for holding a grudge. Even the best of people will make little mistakes, be a little selfish, be a little insensitive. In the great scheme of life, these are small things, and we should let them pass over us, and always run back and make friends, no matter who was 'at fault'.

And in the spirit of friendship, or when we feel that we do need to say something about these little slights to clear the air, dogs once again can provide a good lesson: never bite when a simple growl will do.

* * *

None of us have all the heaven we want.

— Donald McCaig, *Eminent Dogs, Dangerous Men*

IV

Be happy with who you are

Dogs cannot change the fact that they are dogs. They also cannot change how big they are, how they look, or even any of their surroundings. Yet it's hard to imagine that they are constantly worried about their size, their physical looks, or what things look like around them. It's also hard to imagine that they spend any time at all comparing themselves to other dogs.

Of course, we do this all the time, and generally for all the wrong reasons. We compare our looks, our weight, our hairstyle and color – all superficial things. We take these comparisons to an absurd level when we compare *possessions* – what we have versus what other people have, such as a different car, or home, or just different *things*.

And if we do manage to have more than those around us – whether it be more possessions, or better looks, or even better qualities, why should we point this out to others? It isn't our job to tell others how to be better, or to decide for them how they should compare themselves to us (even for good reasons); that we should leave up to them, and just let ourselves be examples, as we can see others around us and learn from them. As Roy Blout has beautifully captured, dogs don't point out or brag about anything that they do better than we do:

> *...yet my heart*
> *(Courage and also affection-wise),*
> *As any fool can see in my eyes,*
> *Is larger than yours, and purer, and yet*
> *I don't make a point of it...*

> — Roy Blout, *If Only You Knew How Much I Smell You: True Portraits of Dogs*

Have you noticed that when you ask someone "How are you?" they usually say they are "Fine" but then always add some mitigating comment, like "I've had this cold" or "Busy!" or "Okay, but I'm tired of dealing with my stupid boss" or something else that seems to imply that their lives are *harder* than yours. As if life were a competition, and it is a battle to just be "Fine" and there's something wrong with being happy.

Dogs don't do this – they show you exactly how they feel and don't try to mask it or make it out to be more than it is. You won't see a dog start to wag its tail, and then suddenly stop as if to say "Well, I'm not *that* happy."

In fact, an important part of achieving happiness with who you are is to express yourself. Dogs never hesitate to show their feelings or ask for what they want. When they see you they wag their tail, when they are relaxed and happy they smile, when given food they are grateful. They don't stifle yawns when tired. Instead they take a nap, and have no shame in needing rest. And when they do something that they know is wrong, they look sheepish and apologetic, admitting their guilt. In short, they are totally honest in revealing their wants, their needs, their limitations, and their mistakes.

On the other hand, we often hide our true feelings, and often hesitate to express our wishes and desires. They stay bottled up inside, sometimes making us resent those around us when they can't discern our feelings and needs. This in turn makes us unhappy, not only with our friends but with ourselves, because we are not 'getting what we want.' Haven't you ever had the experience where you dreaded asking for something, spending a lot of time and mental energy worried about what the reaction would be, and then when you finally said it or asked for it, it turned out not to be a big deal? We sometimes think that others are spending all their time thinking about us, when in fact people tend to think mostly about themselves and what is happening in their lives (which is not necessarily bad at all, this might just be the self preservation part of human nature).

So what if we express ourselves honestly, and accept ourselves for who we are? Does this mean we must stay the same? What happens if we look at ourselves and do not like some of the things that we find?

Here is where we can actually be a bit better off than dogs, because there are things that we can change about ourselves – important things, like our attitudes, our morals, and our personality – in short, many of the characteristics which make us human. Think of how we can become better just by watching how those around us treat other people. We can see the effects of both inconsiderate and considerate people and actions, and learn from both. We can see examples of this all around us: humility, honor, truthfulness, compassion. Unlike dogs, we do have the power to become better.

> *No matter what . . . throws you off balance, there is one guiding principle you could introduce to restore your equilibrium. Just remind yourself of "enough."*
>
> *"Enough" means, "I'm good enough. I own enough. I know enough. I'm smart enough, pretty enough . . . ."*
>
> *"Enough" encourages an inner feeling of peace, an acceptance. It acknowledges that, indeed, there is more out there to have, to be, to own, to achieve, and you are allowed to feel happy and satisfied without having it, being it, owning it, or achieving it.*
>
> *Don't confuse satisfaction with settling. "Enough" is not permission to avoid risk or resist change... "Enough" does not mean, "Give up." It means, "Savor what you've got."*
>
> — Judith Sills, PhD., *Excess Baggage*

This sounds like a contradiction – saying to "Be happy with who you are" but also saying to "Change for the better." Yet if you really think about it, it is not much of a contradiction, because the things to be happy about and accept are the superficial things that don't really matter and that we cannot change anyway, while the things we should change are the things that not only matter, but are the things we *can* change. We can't change the family we've been born into or the genes we've inherited, but we can change what we choose to do with our traits and how we treat other people.

Dr. Sills points out that the acceptance of who we are and what we have also helps lead to a serenity, an 'inner peace.' It does not mean that we cannot grow, and continually contribute to ourselves and others.

There is a well-known prayer that begins "God grant me the serenity to accept the things I cannot change, the courage to change the things I can, and the wisdom to know the difference." Dogs have been granted this very serenity, courage, and wisdom, and we have been granted dogs. We only need to look at them to see how powerful these qualities can be.

* * *

People fret
About "seeking their bliss"
It doesn't get
Any better than this.

— Roy Blout, *If Only You Knew How Much I Smell You:*
True Portraits of Dogs, Valerie Shaff (Photographer)

V

Live for today

In his book *Dogs Never Lie About Love*, Jeffrey Moussaieff Masson talks of how humans tend to judge things, and always compare the present with an idealized past. A friend admonishes him for his habit: "Why do you compare one beach to another? You are here now; enjoy it for what it is."

Isn't it amazing how often we do this? Instead of really looking at and enjoying what is right in front of us, we are constantly comparing our experiences to what happened in the past, or to what we think should happen. Sometimes we even compare it to an idealized image we have in our own minds. Doing this will almost certainly guarantee that we will be disappointed, because 'reality' will never meet our perfect expectations. Yet even knowing this we do it all the time. As Roy Blout says in his poem, people are constantly "fretting" about seeking bliss and perfection, instead of appreciating what they have, and appreciating life itself.

We tend to let this way of thinking affect our relationships as well. We compare our relationships to perfect TV and Hollywood-created images of perfect couples, perfect marriages, perfect families, perfect friends. Next to these images, the reality of life falls short, and what gets highlighted are the shortcomings, not the beauty of what we already have and opportunities that we can create.

We'll never know whether dogs ever think in terms of 'comparisons,' but as we watch a dog chew merrily on a bone, it's hard to imagine he is thinking "it's too bad this bone isn't as good as the one I had last week!" Instead, he seems to get 100 percent enjoyment out of that bone. In the same way, as a dog rolls around on the grass, he doesn't seem to be comparing his experience (and limiting his obvious joy) to another patch of grass or a prior experience. Dogs will exercise in any place, in any weather, in total enjoyment. People, on the other hand, are more likely to drive to a gym – and then complain about the surroundings.

Dogs always seem to be living not only in the day, but in the moment. Have you ever noticed how especially excited they seem in the morning to get out and do something? It's as if they are saying "Let's go! Today is my favorite day, and it's here!"

> *"It's Today!" Squeaked Piglet.*
> *"My favorite day." Said Pooh.*
> — Benjamin Hoff, *The Tao of Pooh*

Unlike Pooh, we seem to spend a lot of time each day worrying about tomorrow, or re-living yesterday. When we do meet someone like Pooh, they seem so, well, refreshing, as if their favorite day is *today*. You can see it in their attitudes, how they approach what they do every day, how they interact with the people around them, and how they think about their lives.

The next time you are on vacation, or just at some popular place like a nice beach or a park or looking at a mountain view, stop and watch what everyone else there is doing. It's amazing how many people, no matter how beautiful the spot, merely show up, look around quickly, take a photo, and leave. They spend more time worrying about how to capture an image on film ("John, move over a bit to the right!") than they do really looking at what is right in front of them. Very few people seem to really immerse themselves and experience it for what it is, right there. You might try leaving your camera behind on your next visit somewhere, and see how it affects your experience, your pleasure, and your memories of the event.

Betty Smith said: "Look at everything as if you were seeing it for the first or last time. Then your time on earth will be filled with glory." It's easy to 'fill' your life now, with worries, stress, activities, and *stuff*. You can easily have a very filled-up life without living a full life, or being fulfilled. The first step to fulfillment is to live the day that is right in front of you – today.

Now, we can't totally ignore the past and the future. We have a history, and responsibilities, and bills to pay (and dogs to feed!). But it's easy to spend so much time thinking about yesterday and worrying about tomorrow that we get little enjoyment out of the beauty and the reality of every day.

Taken to the extreme, this constant worry and planning leads to a life of 'incrementalization' where we are constantly planning for the future, and saying "Once I finish this thing, *then* I can really start to live." Think of all the people you know who go to college, and then say "Now I'll work hard for two years in my first job; I know I'll have to sacrifice and not really enjoy life because I have to pay my dues." Then after they do that (and it stretches to 3 years) they say "I need to go back to school so I can get a better job; I'll really take it seriously this time, it'll only be for a few years, and then I can get a better paying, easier job." And after that is done they say "Well, I'll work hard at this job for a few years, and get my career established, and then I can slow down and relax." Then they think "It's time to get married, I'd better get serious about that." And then – well, you get the idea. It's not that each of these things aren't great things to do in and of themselves, or one at a time, or together. But life can easily become a series of independent 'steps' that consume all energy, all with the goal of getting to the point where we can 'start living.' Some people never reach this point, because their entire life always has 'one more thing to do.' Others think this is what 'retirement' is for, but if you ask retired people who are enjoying life what they most wish for, they say "I should have done this 30 years ago!"

In *The Tao of Pooh*, Benjamin Hoff says that our "religions, sciences, and business ethics have tried their hardest to convince us that there is a Great Reward waiting for us somewhere, and that what we have to do is spend our lives working like lunatics to catch up with it. Whether it's up in the sky, behind the next molecule, or in the executive suite, it's somehow always farther along than we are — just down the road, on the other side of the world, past the moon, beyond the stars . . . " In fact, our "Great Reward" is right here in front of us – it's living, being able to experience every day.

Someone once said that life is not a dress rehearsal. We only get one crack at it. Unlike a play at the theater, we don't have to follow a script, or worry about making a mistake. What we do have to accept is that we only get to do it once.

You might think that the reason dogs enjoy every day is that they have a relatively short life. But the dogs probably don't know this. If dogs lived to be 100, they'd probably just have that many more days to live to their fullest. While we all wonder what heaven is going to be like, dogs live it.

* * *

Through the window beyond the mirror I see there is a porch out back, and when done go out and stand on it. It's at a level with the tops of the trees surrounding the hotel which seem to respond to this morning air the same way I do. The branches and leaves move with each light breeze as if it were expected, were what had been waited for all this time.

— Robert M. Pirsig, *Zen and the Art of Motorcycle Maintenance*

VI

Go with the flow

Dogs are tremendously flexible creatures. While they have their own personalities and perhaps preferences, they have an amazing ability to take what they are presented with and not only live with it but make the most of it. If a dog lies down on a rug and you take away the rug, he looks for another warm and soft spot on which to lie. Failing to find that, he lies on the hard floor. He doesn't spend time whining about why you took the rug away. Put down a bowl of food, take it away and replace it with different (even if not as 'tasty') food, and if he's still hungry he'll eat that. It's as if dogs just go with the flow of life, take what is before them, and enjoy it for what it is.

We often have a hard time doing this. We constantly push back when anything doesn't go exactly our way, instead of making the most (and improving upon) what we have. We spend a lot of time blaming others because our life isn't perfect or because we don't have every little thing that we want or feel that we need. This blaming and pushing back is often indirect – we can't (or aren't willing to) confront the person or thing that we feel is to blame for the shortcomings in our life, and we spend a lot of time, energy, and stress in placing blame and complaining. (Think of why a lot of people gossip – it's to 'get back' at someone who has caused them some pain, or of whom they are jealous).

At times, we spend so much time dodging and weaving that we hit more obstacles than we avoid.

Some people think that going with the flow is the same as having no direction and living an aimless life. This does not have to be the case at all. Just as we can 'live today' and still learn from our experiences of 'yesterday' and remember the responsibilities of 'tomorrow,' we can have a goal and purpose in life and yet approach those goals and purposes in many different ways. One way is to always battle for everything, to argue every point, to make sure we win every contest. In short, to live a life of constant resistance and stress. When we do this, no matter how much we plan ahead, isn't it amazing how often things don't go 'our way,' or that things 'go wrong,' or in general aren't easy?

The other way, of course, is to have a direction, but to choose the path – and the way of walking the path – that deals with life in a way that minimizes conflict. Everything does not have to be a battle. Some of the most potentially difficult things can just pass painlessly by if we have the right attitude.

Have you ever noticed what happens when you go to a store to return a product that is broken, or for which you lost the receipt? If you go in with an attitude of 'demanding your money back' or 'it's the store's fault,' you are likely to get a surly response and no satisfaction (or if you do, it's only after a very stressful confrontation). But when you admit that you lost the receipt, or have a general attitude of asking for help, you are much more likely to get a good response and good service. Same situation, but your attitude leads to a totally different result. In the same way, if you have to deal with someone who is unpleasant, responding in kind only makes it worse, but a softer response (or even avoidance) usually has a much better effect.

Like dogs, we can go with the flow and do the best with what we have. And unlike dogs, we can do this while at the same time having a purpose and a goal in life – a purpose and goal that we choose for ourselves. Robert Pirsig is writing about the Zen-like way in which the trees seem to be actually waiting for the breeze, so that that they can move with it, going with its flow. We, too, can ready ourselves and be a part of the flow around us, the flow of activity, of experiences, of life.

When the wind moves the branches, dogs always seem to be in the right spot to feel the freshness of the air.

* * *

It wasn't a matter of courage or dreams, but something a whole lot simpler. A pilot would call it ground orientation. I'd spent a long time circling above the clouds, looking for life, while Hallie was living it.

— Barbara Kingsolver, *Animal Dreams*

VII

Life is the journey itself

Like the character in Barbara Kingsolver's book, dogs live life, they don't waste time looking for it. Sometimes we spend so much time trying to find out exactly where we should be going that we don't realize where we are now or even when we've arrived.

One of the enemies of sound, lifelong motivation is a rather childish conception we have of the kind of concrete, describable goal toward which all of our efforts drive us. We want to believe that there is a point at which we can feel that we have arrived. We want a scoring system that tells us when we've piled up enough points to count ourselves successful.

So you scramble and sweat and climb to reach what you thought was the goal. When you get to the top you stand up and look around and chances are you feel a little empty. Maybe more than a little empty.

You wonder whether you climbed the wrong mountain.

But life isn't a mountain that has a summit. Nor is it — as some suppose — a riddle that has an answer. Nor a game that has a final score.

Life is an endless unfolding, and if we wish it to be, an endless process of self-discovery, an endless and unpredictable dialogue between our own potentialities and the life situations in which we find ourselves.

— John Gardner *(from a speech on Personal Renewal)*

Have you ever watched a puppy or even an older dog see or experience something for the first time? This is a good example of the "endless unfolding" of which John Gardner speaks. All of the dog's emphasis and attention is focused on what is right in front of it. The dog doesn't seem to be thinking or worrying about how its new experience fits into its overall goal in life. Instead, it just focuses all its attention on the new experience.

This doesn't mean that we shouldn't have goals, or that we should not keep our goals in mind as we go about our everyday lives. In fact, our goals can actually enrich our everyday experiences and help us enjoy the journey that is life. As Benjamin Hoff writes in *The Tao of Pooh:*

That doesn't mean that the goals we have don't count. They do, mostly because they cause us to go through the process, and it's the process that makes us wise, happy, or whatever. If we do things in the wrong sort of way, it makes us miserable, angry, confused, and things like that. The goal has to be right for us, and it has to be beneficial, in order to ensure a beneficial process. But aside from that, it's really the process that's important. Enjoyment of the process is the secret that erases the myths of the Great Reward and Saving Time.

— Benjamin Hoff, *The Tao of Pooh*

The key point here, and one that dogs seem to understand, is that the process itself (life) is what we should be enjoying. In essence, perhaps, one of our goals in life should be to enjoy life itself. Wouldn't this be the ultimate self-fulfilling and life improving goal? Frederico Fellini said, "There is no end. There is no beginning. There is only the infinite passion of life."

This doesn't mean that we can't have other important goals. But even these goals should be thought of as a process. This will not only help us to enjoy and learn from the experiences we have in striving for our goals, but it will help us keep from being disappointed if we do not reach some exact "end point" that we defined.

Have you ever noticed that when you set very high expectations for something, whether it be a movie, or a job, or a relationship, you tend to be disappointed, but when you instead concentrate on the experience (instead of the expectation or the goal) you tend to enjoy the movie more, like the job better, or have more fun in the relationship? This is the real world of life's journey – when we get too focused on some specific end point, we are bound to be disappointed (either because we don't reach it exactly, or because we did not have the ability to pre-define what it should be). But when we concentrate on the process of reaching our goal, we learn along the way, and the entire journey is the fulfillment of the goal. In short, we don't waste any of our life on the way to what we think life should be.

Most importantly, enjoying the process and making it in itself a goal helps us to focus our lives on what really is important.

> *Just to observe where your time goes and what you are preoccupied with is a wonderful mindfulness practice in itself. The risk comes down to the possibility that your whole life could go by and you would miss it — because you were absorbed in those things that you thought you really needed to be doing, and you weren't examining the choices you are making. To be awake while you're on the cushion and in your everyday life is invaluable.*

> —Jon Kabat-Zinn (interview with Andrew Weil)

Thinking of life as only the time consuming path to a goal is like the peril of 'incrementalization.' If you find yourself saying "I just need to do one more thing before I can…" then there is a good chance you are not getting the most out of life. Instead, you might want to think "I can have fun while I…" or, at the least, like dogs, put 100 percent of your attention into what you do, instead of worrying about how everything you do fits into your overall plan for life.

If you were to describe to someone what your dog means to you, your description would probably not include some goal the dog helped you reach. Rather, you would say that your dog brought you happiness, and was fun, and a good companion, and that you did things together. In other words, your dog is part of the journey of your life, not the achievement of some goal. And if your dog could describe *you*, he would certainly do it the same way.

A process is not a straight line, it's a rich set of inter-related actions, choices, and experiences. So we should not expect our goals, happiness, and life itself to be somewhere 'out there' or 'coming after something,' but instead be attainable every day. Life isn't something to be reached tomorrow; it is something to be experienced today.

* * *

There are two ways of spreading the light; to be the candle or the mirror that reflects it.

— Edith Wharton

VIII

Make the world a better place

The best way to make the world a better place is to first realize that you can:

> *A wonderful realization will be the day you realize that you are unique in all the world. There is nothing that is an accident. You are a special combination for a purpose — and don't let them tell you otherwise, even if they tell you that purpose is an illusion. (Live an illusion if you have to.) You are that combination so that you can do what is essential for you to do. Don't ever believe that you have nothing to contribute. The world is an incredible unfulfilled tapestry, and only you can fulfill that tiny space that is yours.*
> — Leo F. Buscaglia, PhD., *Living, Loving and Learning*

Dr. Buscaglia is saying that though the world is a big place, you are an important person, and you can make an essential contribution to it. But even if you realize that you can make the world a better place, you may wonder how, exactly, can you do this?

There are many ways.

First, you can do things that *matter*. This can mean helping others, creating something, being a good parent, worker, dog trainer, whatever. Most important, though, is that *you* should be the one to decide whether it matters or not. It must matter to you – if it doesn't, it isn't likely to matter to anyone else (no matter what they say) and you won't be able to do it 100 percent (like dogs do!) because you won't have your heart in it. Confucius said "Wheresoever you go, go with all your heart." By this he means where you go with your life and what you do. You can help make not only your world better, but everyone else's as well.

> *You have your brush and your colors. You paint paradise, and in you go.*
> — Nicos Kazantzakis

And you don't need to think your way to what matters, or be especially clever. Usually what you need to do is right in front of you. Thinking too much about it is more likely to lead you into a complicated set of plans in your mind, which aren't likely to come true anyway, resulting in disappointment.

> *The ways are simple, we have made them seem complicated.*
> — Robert James Waller, *The Bridges of Madison County*

Second, since we can't all be the ones 'out in front' with new creations and new ideas, we can certainly help others along, whether they be leaders or followers. As Edith Wharton says, there are two ways of "spreading the light" and making the world a better place. If we can't be the candle, we can be the mirror, helping, reflecting, and strengthening those who are doing good.

John Gardner said "Some people make the world a better place just by being in it." This is something that dogs seem to do. They make us happy by just being, well, dogs. (If you have a dog, think of how many times your dog has made you feel better just by being there). If we do things that matter to us, and surround ourselves with good people, in the end, without trying (or just by going with the flow) we'll contribute to making the world a better place – just by being in it. In this regard, like attracts like. If we contribute to making the world a better place, wherever we can, then others will emerge that will help reflect our good deeds and our light.

Some people are afraid to try to do the things that might make the world better, because they feel that they will have to change their lives, or take risks. For those afraid, they should remember that the journey of life includes both risks and failures. As Dr. Judith Sills says:

> *Achievement, toward whatever goal, is a mountain we climb. So many people spend their lifetimes tucked safely into a valley at the base of that mountain, dreaming of life on top. The people who*

live at the top did not get there because they failed less on the way.
They got there because they were willing to endure more failure.

— Judith Sills, PhD., *Excess Baggage*

Of course, once at the top of the mountain, there is usually another hill to climb that you could not see, either from the base or even along the way to what you thought was the top. This is why life and goals should not be thought of as a finite end point, but as a process. Climbing the mountain will in itself make you a better person, and will in turn make the world a better place. Your achievement doesn't have to be a cure for cancer, or solving world hunger. Instead, by making yourself a better person, you will contribute to making the world better, both as an individual and as a source of support and 'reflecting power' for others.

In the end, no matter what you do, do it with passion. Some people go their entire lives without once ever feeling passionately about anything. Maybe they are afraid of all the emotion. Don't be afraid of passion, embrace it. Passion brings energy. Those around you will feel it and be motivated by it, and in turn it will help them motivate others.

Making the world a better place is to be successful in a way that is far greater and more important than success in a job, a sport, or any single activity:

> *To laugh often and much; to win the respect of*
> *intelligent people and the affection of children; to earn the*
> *appreciation of honest critics and endure the betrayal of false*

beauty, to find the best in others; to leave the world a bit better, whether by a healthy child, a garden patch or a redeemed social condition; to know even one life has breathed easier because you lived.
   This is to have succeeded.

— Emerson

And for the people who feel that they need to change too much, or that it is hard to make the world better just by being themselves, just take a look at dogs once again. They can't give donations, feed the poor, or invent new medications. In fact, they usually aren't trying to *do* anything, but they make the world a better place anyway, just by being who they are.

* * *

People hate to grow old when they didn't do what they wanted when they were young.

— Donald McCaig, *Eminent Dogs, Dangerous Men*

IX

Have fun!

Just as we can make the world a better place by doing
things that matter, we can also best be happy by doing the
things we are excited about – in other words, things that we
think are fun. Most of the regrets people have in life are that
they didn't have enough fun. They don't regret the things they
did, but rather what they *didn't do*. Think about the things that
you regret, even if you are relatively young. Most of your regrets
are probably things that you didn't say, didn't do, didn't see.
And if you really examine why you 'regret' these missing things,
it's likely that it's because they would have been fun to do.

Dogs don't seem to have regrets. There seems to be two
reasons for this. First, they live for today. It's hard to be
regretting the past when your full attention is focused on the
present. And it's especially hard to regret the past when you
don't spend a lot of time dwelling on what might have been.

Try filing the past where it belonged instead of running it back
and forth like some tape you could edit to spec.

— Richard Barre, *Blackheart Highway*

Second, dogs seem to try to do things that are fun as often as they can. This also makes it hard to have lots of regrets about not doing things, because if you spend most of your life doing the things you want to do, then you won't have a whole lot of things that you wanted to do but didn't.

Jean Donaldson sees dogs following a marvelously simplistic approach to life:

> *There are two kinds of things that happen in life, good things*
> *and bad things, so there are four kinds of consequences: good*
> *stuff can 1) start and 2) end. Bad stuff can 1) start and 2)*
> *end. Your dog is constantly trying to start the good stuff, end*
> *the bad stuff, avoid ending the good stuff and avoid starting*
> *the bad stuff.*

— Jean Donaldson, *The Culture Clash*

What a wonderfully simplistic set of rules for living! Think of how much better your life would be if you followed these simple 'rules.' Yet, it often seems that we do just the opposite – we don't initiate enough 'good stuff' ("I don't have time to take a walk…read a book…take a vacation"). We also don't proactively and single-mindedly try to end 'the bad stuff.' Think of how often we let things go on that aren't good for us – staying in a bad job, or a bad relationship, or maintaining an unhealthy lifestyle, or spending too much time with people who don't create a 'net positive' in our lives. We let the bad stuff drag on way too long, even when in many cases we can end some of these things quite easily.

If we did nothing more than focus on starting good things today, *now* (not tomorrow or next week) and ending the unpleasant things today, *now* (not tomorrow or next week) our lives would be much happier. It's not that you need to have a grand plan, just that you make the decision (and act on it) to stop the bad and start the good. Yogi Berra said "If you don't know where you are going, you might wind up someplace else." This might not be all bad, as long as the someplace else is a better place than you are now – and you enjoy the journey along the way.

Now, all of this focus doesn't mean that you have to be too serious about the whole thing. Have you ever seen people working so hard to have fun that they seem miserable? Or where the fun is so planned that if something doesn't go according to the plan, the fun is lost?

> *During break time at obedience school, two dogs were talking. One said to the other... "The thing I hate about obedience school is you learn ALL this stuff you'll never use in the real world."*

When my friends come to visit, one of the dogs will often bring them a ball to throw. After throwing the ball, the person often apologizes with something like "Sorry! I can't throw so well." Meanwhile the dog is off happily chasing the ball. *The dog doesn't care about how well you throw.* He's having fun and not worried about it being perfect, so why should you?

The important thing to remember is that you should just do more of the good stuff in life, and make sure you are doing whatever you can to end the bad stuff. You don't have to have it all planned out; you just need to do it.

Once you are on this path, it gets better and better (sort of a self-fulfilling process) because the marginal things in your life will constantly fall by the wayside, and instead more and more of your time will be filled with the things that you can be happy and excited about. This doesn't mean that there won't be chores to do, and that all 'un-fun' things will be eliminated. But the emphasis will clearly shift, and your real priorities will become clearer.

Charles Kingsley said, "We act as though comfort and luxury were the chief requirements in life, when all that we need to make us really happy is something to be enthusiastic about." Have you noticed that people who are enthusiastic about things often seem to have 'fun' lives? It's almost as if they don't have time for bad stuff, because they have no time for it.

In the end, there will be another reward. By doing the good and fun things, you will be happier, and this will be evident to others, drawing more positive people to you. Content people cannot hide their happiness. It is obvious and infectious, just like it is in dogs:

> *Dogs are lousy poker players. When the get a good hand they wag their tails.*

* * *

Dogs are notorious for hope. Dogs believe that this morning may begin a day of fascination, easily grander than any day in the past. Perhaps the work did go badly yesterday, perhaps the humans are wild with sulks and rages, but this morning can yet be saved: don't humans understand anything?

Every morning, in dog pounds all over America, hundreds of dogs awake to their last day with gladness in their hearts.

— Donald McCaig, *Nop's Hope*

X

Have everlasting and absolute faith

So here we are at the 10th Canine Commandment. Maybe we've learned something from dogs, and taken it to heart. Even if we don't want to make big changes in our lives, maybe we'll just stop from time to time and think about another way of doing certain things. Or maybe we'll just look at dogs a little differently when we see them next.

Of course, we should never really try to be totally like dogs – after all, while we've done all this exploring of how we might be better by learning from them, at the end of the day we are more complex beings, with more responsibilities, and have the (unfortunate) sense of time. What happens now means something different because of what happened yesterday, and we cannot divorce what happened yesterday from what may happen tomorrow.

But just because we cannot transcend into something that is human but with all the good qualities of dog life, we can still benefit from the new way of looking at life that dogs can show us. It won't make our lives perfect, but that doesn't make it any less helpful. Some people, after trying a diet and finding that it doesn't make them thin overnight, give up. In our case, maybe you might try to look at life a little differently now, but if you don't achieve overnight 'happiness' you might give up as well. This might be a greater loss than not trying to change at all. For the power to change is something that we can do that dogs really cannot. And if they could, I doubt whether they would make this mistake. They would simply keep trying to get better – just as when they smell a bone under the couch they won't give up until they find a way to get it out.

Dogs, you see, have everlasting and absolute faith:

There is no faith which has never yet been broken, except that of a truly faithful dog.

- Konrad Lorenz

It's this faith that keeps dogs the way they are – the faith that *today* will be a great day, that bad things will end, that good things will happen, that no matter what went wrong yesterday, today is another day to enjoy life, another day to make friends, another day to be happy, another day to live.

Dogs have the ability, so rare in humans, to be always and continuously feeling their own internal emotions. This is so apparent that it must play no small role in our love for dogs. At the same time, if a dog grows up in a loving home, the dog will not experience unhappiness and will not develop into an unhappy animal, one prone to sadness or what we think about as neurosis. Even if the dog has had his share of misery in the past — and here is the great lesson we can take from dogs — he somehow manages, without the benefit of analysis, to overcome the past, to emerge from a time of sorrow with a strange kind of optimism.

— Jeffrey Moussaieff Masson, *Dogs Never Lie About Love.*

And this should be our most important lesson. Nothing will make us more likely to have fun, peaceful, and happy lives than the absolute faith that it is possible for us to do so.

After all, dogs do it every day.

* * *

This story is true, except for the parts that haven't happened yet.

After

My name is Rocco, and I am the luckiest dog in the world. I live with the best family. Besides me, there is Iris, who is also a dog. I've heard that she is a Golden Retriever, whatever that means; maybe it's because she is gold and fluffy. And there's Roy, who is a Border Collie. Me, I've heard that I am a mutt, a collieshephard, and that's just fine with me. I'm brown and black and have white paws. The other members of the family are Cindy and Rick. They are both humans, and they are a lot of fun. I don't know if they are mutts or collieshephards or retrievers, but it doesn't matter to me.

I first met Iris at the dog pound. My earliest memories, in fact, are of waking up one day, my nose wet, my head resting on top of another dog, warm and comfortable. I later found out that her name was Iris, and we became instant friends. I was just a puppy, but Iris didn't seem to mind even though she was a real dog. There were other dogs in the pen, and they were fun too, but there was something special about Iris. She must have felt the same way about me, because even with all the other dog sounds and smells, sometimes I felt that it was just me and Iris there.

Me and Iris would chase each other around the pen. Well, I would chase Iris, and she would run away. And then I would stop and run away, and Iris would turn and chase me. I could never catch Iris, but she could catch me whenever she wanted. Right away, we had a lot in common. We both liked to run around, explore the outside of the pen, and play with the other dogs. We even ate out of the same bowl. At night we would sleep close together, our bodies intertwined.

Every so often people would come to the dog pound and sometimes they would take one of the dogs away. Even though I missed the dog that left, for some reason it always made me happy too. Some days I'd wake up thinking: "Maybe this will be the day that someone will come for me and Iris."

We also had a friend in the next pen, which was separated from ours by a fence. Her name was Keltri, and when Iris and I would chase each other around, she would bark encouragement. Even though she was not in the same pen with us, we were still close to her, and I know that she was glad that Iris and I had fun together.

One day, the man who fed us came and stood in front of Keltri's pen, and said, "Well, this is your last week. I hope somebody comes for some of you." He sounded sad. Then he went over to the pen at the very end of the room, where there was only one very old dog, who I did not know because he was so far away. There had been other dogs in that pen, but the man had taken them away. The man opened the door of the pen, and I expected the old dog to run out, because we always liked to do that when the door was opened. But the old dog just lay there. The man tried to get him to come out, but the dog did not seem to want to go, and finally the man had to go in and pick him up. He said, "Sorry, old fella, it's time." He carried the old dog out and through another door at the back of the room. I didn't know where that went since I had never been there. We didn't pay too much attention anyway, because we were together, although when I heard that door close I suddenly didn't feel like playing anymore, so I just sat down. So did Iris and Keltri. We never saw the old dog again.

* * *

I first met Rick a few days later. He came in with the man, and I liked him right away. He went from pen to pen, and when he got to Keltri's pen he bent down to be near the dogs, and put his face up against the wire fence. I always liked when humans did that, so I could be close to them and smell them and feel their warm breath and if I listened closely I could even hear their heart beat (dogs have very good ears). Rick played with some of the dogs (he seemed to like Keltri, and since I liked Keltri too, it made me like Rick even more) through the screen, and actually went in to Keltri's pen, and I could tell that all of the dogs really liked him, because they all stopped playing with each other, or woke up, or stopped eating, and they all tried to jump on him and get close to him. Even though some humans had taken some of the dogs out of Keltri's pen over the last few days, it was still crowded and there were about ten dogs there. I had started to get to know some of them too.

After a while Rick stood up and talked to the man, who was waiting outside the pen, and he pointed at Keltri and said her name. I nuzzled up to divider between our pens and Keltri came over to me. I could tell that she liked Rick too, because she was happy. Keltri turned around and barked, and Rick looked at us, and he came over and bent down again and put his hand up against the fence for me to smell.

"Hi," he said, "are you a friend of Keltri's?" I wagged my tail and licked his hand. Iris, always by my side, came up to see Rick too.

"The puppy is Rocco," said the man. "And the retriever is Iris. They're inseparable."

"Were they brought in together?" asked Rick.

"No," said the man. "They just found each other in the pack and hit it off. I've never seen two dogs get so close in a week. It was just luck that they ended up together. If they had come in a just a few days apart, they might be in different pens and would probably never have had so much fun in a place like this."

"Sort of makes you believe in fate, doesn't it?" asked Rick. He stood up. "What happens to these dogs?"

"Well, you know that we can only keep them so long. We hold on to them for nine weeks. See the number on every pen?" He pointed to Keltri's pen. "This is the ninth week for this pen. If no one adopts them by Saturday . . ."

"I see," said Rick. "Do you have to do it?" he asked softly.

"Yeah," said the man. "I hate it, but what are you going to do? We don't have enough money or space to keep them any longer. Most of the puppies get adopted quick, but the older ones. . ." He looked over to the pen where the old dog had been. "I have to move these dogs over there tomorrow. You can't imagine how much I hate Saturdays."

"What happens if there are no dogs in the number 9 pen?" asked Rick.

"Well, I would get a week off, I guess. But it has never happened. Look in there. These dogs have been here for over eight weeks. Usually there are only one or two dogs left by the end of all that time, but for some reason this whole batch came in at once. We aren't going to get ten people adopting these dogs this week. Plus, people who know dogs see how some of them stick together, and won't adopt just one of them. Look at Rocco and Iris. They belong together. Take them apart, and who knows what they would be like."

When the man mentioned my name I went over to the door and looked out at Rick. He came over again and bent down on his knees and scratched me behind the ear. Boy, did I like him! I couldn't explain it, because I had seen a lot of humans before, but he made me feel good, and happy. I wagged my tail madly.

"How much does it cost to adopt a dog?" asked Rick.

"Well, it's 50 dollars for the neutering, and 10 dollars for the adoption fee."

"What do you do with people who adopt a dog and then find out they don't want it? Do you take them back?"

"Oh yes, of course. No decision is irreversible. It happens every so often. Sometimes people aren't sure, but we suggest that they go ahead and try it for a while, because the whole family needs to get comfortable in their new homes. Sometimes the dogs and even the people are afraid at first, especially if they have never done this, but it almost always works if there is a good match and everyone gives it a try. Dogs are very accepting, and people can be too."

"But if one comes back, say from pen 9, what pen does it go in?"

"Well, like I said, it doesn't happen very often, so there are no real rules. But if a dog is adopted once, and gets so close to making it, I couldn't face putting it back into number 9. I usually put it back in number 1."

"Nine more weeks," said Rick.

"Yeah. A lot can happen in nine weeks."

Rick stood up. "Who makes the decisions around here?"

"Well, for adoption, I do. There is a Board, but that's just for the budget and stuff."

"How is the budget?"

"What do you think? We're always broke. At the end of the month, the money sometimes runs out, and we can't buy food. I'm not supposed to feed the dogs in number 9 when that happens, but . . . well, I usually stop at the store and find a way to bring in something myself." The man looked away.

"Okay," said Rick. "Here's the deal, just between you and me. I'll take two of them, that's all I can do." He pointed at me, and I had the urge to jump the fence. "The puppy, Rocco. And since they obviously belong together, Iris too. I need to talk to someone on this, so I want to bring them home and let us all spend some time together. I think after a little time we will all know if it is the right thing for us, although I feel real good about it already."

"Sounds good," said the man. "I was hoping that the two of them would get to be together."

"Okay, let's try something else," said Rick. "You've got ten dogs in pen 9. What if I adopted all of them, but then found out — maybe as soon as I got them outside — that I couldn't get all of them in the car?"

The man was quiet for a moment. "Well," he said slowly, "I guess you'd have to bring them back."

"Yes, but where would they go?"

"I guess they'd go in pen 1. After all, if you brought them back in a week, that's where they'd go. This is all hypothetical, of course. If I knew that you only had a car, or couldn't care for 12 dogs, I wouldn't let you adopt them. Besides, you'd lose your 60 dollars per dog, and we'd have to fill out a bunch of forms."

"Do some people ever come in and can't afford the fee?" Rick asked.

"Sometimes. We try to find dogs that have already been neutered for them, so they don't have to pay for that."

"Lots of work," said Rick. "Filling out the adoption papers, taking all those dogs to the car, finding out they won't fit, bringing them all back, filling out more forms."

"Yeah," said the man. "Lots of work."

"Rocco and Iris, plus ten dogs in number 9. That's twelve dogs at 60 dollars per dog; 720 dollars, is that right?"

"Well, a little less than that. Some of them have already been neutered."

"Okay, let's call it 700 even." He took out his wallet. "What if you didn't know I had a small car, and we just skipped all that part of it, and just took the dogs from number 9, and moved them over to number 1?"

The man thought for a while. "Save a lot of paperwork," he said. "And I could feed a lot of dogs for 700 bucks. What's the catch?"

"I get to move them," said Rick.

And that's exactly what he did. He took the dogs one by one out of the pen next to us, and moved them over to another pen near the door. He left Keltri for last, so she could be near us, and as he picked her up I heard him say "I'll be back for you girl, I promise. Even if you can't live with us, we'll help you find a home close by, so you can always visit."

And he did that too.

* * *

Me and Iris and Roy and Rick and Cindy all live in a big house near a place called Middleburg, but Rick and Cindy always call it home. It has lots of places to run around outside, and we come and go in and out whenever we want. Rick and Cindy take us for long walks through the woods behind the house, and I like to chase squirrels and birds. Iris, Roy and I run ahead along the path, and then have to come back, be- cause Cindy and Rick are slower than we are.

By the time we came to live here, Roy had been with Rick and Cindy for a long time. I thought at first that he might be jealous, since we were new, but he accepted us from the start and let us know what a good time we were going to have. Oh, of course every so often we did something that maybe wasn't quite right, like try to play too hard, or bother him when he was really tired (he was sometimes a working dog, you see). But he wouldn't really get mad, maybe just give us a tiny growl to let us know how he felt, and then all would be forgotten.

There's a big porch in back of the house, and it overlooks the old farm that we live on, and the hills and woods. I love to lie on the porch in the summer, right outside the wooden screen door (that Roy taught me how to open from the inside; I'm always learning fun things from him) because from here I can see everything that goes on. The kitchen is right there, and I can hear the refrigerator door open, which usually means a snack for me. I can also look through the opening in the porch railing into the yard, and can see whether Cindy or Rick are coming home. I can recognize the sound of their cars from a long way away, and I trot down to the end of the driveway to wait for them when I hear the car.

So this spot right on the porch is kind of mine. Cindy used to say that I was always in the way here, right outside the door, but I don't think she minds, since she put a rug out for me right where I lie down. During the day I sleep there because it is nice and cool.

When I'm not on the porch, I sometimes wander down to one of the barns to visit Revi and Arbetta. They are horses and live in the big red barn with the white trim in the back of the house. They are a little big to play with, even though I'm grown up now, but since they can't come up to the house, I try to check up on them every so often.

When I first met Revi and Arbetta I was a little afraid, because I had never seen a horse before and they were so big. I think Iris was a little afraid too, but when we are together I always felt that we could do anything, and that's how I got to try a lot of new things. And Roy was really helpful, because he showed us what to do and how not to get in the way. After a while we all felt much better, and now we are all friends. It's great when Rick and Cindy ride, because me and Iris and Roy get to run alongside and get a good sweat going. Sometimes they ride really fast, and we can't keep up, so we sit and wait for them to come back.

When I'm not on the porch, or running around, or by the barn, I'm in the house. It's an old white farmhouse that's fun to explore. In the living room, there's another rug in front of the fireplace, which Cindy lights almost every day. This is Iris' favorite place, lying in front of the fire. You can hear the refrigerator door from here too if you listen really good.

At night, Rick sits in a big black chair in front of the fireplace, and Cindy usually sits close by on the floor, her back against the sofa. This puts her partially on Iris rug, but she doesn't mind, and I usually curl up there too, and every so often Cindy or Rick reach over and give us a scratch.

The bedroom is in the back of the house, upstairs, and it has its own porch. When I first moved here, I wasn't allowed in the bedroom, and there was a small fence in the doorway to keep me out, which Rick put up one day and told me that it was to keep me away from Ralph Lauren's sheets, whoever he is. I couldn't understand this, because I would be with Rick and Cindy all day, but at night I couldn't be with them. So I used to whine a little, so Rick took a blanket off the bed and put it right outside the bedroom door. It smelled like Cindy and Rick, and that made be feel better, and so I would sleep in the hall. Rick always made some comment about having a designer blanket for a dog, which would make Cindy laugh (she was always laughing) but I didn't understand. After a while I learned that they would never be far away, and I got used to it, and was able to sleep.

But one night when I was still a pup there was a big storm, and the house lit up with lightning, and the thunder hurt my ears. I had never heard thunder before, and I was confused, and very afraid. Rick came out in the hall to pet me for a while, and that helped, but every time the thunder boomed my eyes would get big and I would start to shake.

Rick sat down and held me close and talked to me. "I'm here Rocco, don't be afraid," he said. But Cindy came over and took me from his arms and carried me to the bed and lay me down on it. Rick and Cindy crawled in, and they fit really close together, so there was plenty of room for me. I snuggled up on top of the covers, and I could feel their warm bodies, and hear them talking, and finally I felt safe, and so I fell asleep. Thunder never bothered me after that, because I always knew that Rick would be there to hold me, and Cindy would carry me to a warm and comfortable place.

* * *

Most of the time Rick and Cindy are at home together, but every so often they would be away, and one of their friends would come over to take care of us. They were very nice, but it wasn't the same when Cindy and Rick weren't there. Even if they were not in the same room, I knew they were around, and that made me feel better. I know Iris and Roy felt the same way, because we were always a little mopey when we were alone, and we slept a lot then. But we always knew that they would come back to us, so we weren't worried.

Roy especially seemed to miss Rick, because they had been together for a long time, from even before Rick met Cindy, I think. Roy would do anything for Rick if he could, and Rick would do anything for Roy. I once heard someone call Roy "Loyal" and I didn't know if that was another name for him, but if it was I'd be happy if someone called me Loyal too.

Sometimes Rick would be gone and Cindy would be at home, or Cindy would be gone and Rick would be there. It was good that Roy and Iris and me were around to keep them company, because I knew that they missed each other. When this happened they would always talk on the phone a lot, and I could tell if Cindy was talking to Rick because she would carry the phone over to the fireplace and lean back on the sofa in her favorite place and scratch me absently (which was just fine with me) while she talked to him. I know this sounds strange but I would swear that her hands were warmer when she was talking to Rick, and I could hear her voice change and her heart beat faster, and she laughed a lot, and sometimes mentioned one of our names, and we would thump our tails on the rug, hoping he would hear.

* * *

Lots of times people would come to visit, and that was always fun. Cindy's Mom and Dad would come, and so would Rick's Mom and Dad, and sometimes we would all sit out on the porch, and there would always be lots of food, which meant lots of leftovers for us. Both Cindy's Dad and Rick's Dad liked to do things around the yard, but they would always stop to pet me. I would follow them around, and when they stayed for a while in one place, like in the garden, I would find a nice warm spot and fall asleep in the sun, and when I awoke I would look around for everyone, and if they were not there I'd sniff them out and move to a new spot. Sometimes when this happened Rick's Dad would call me a "JustlikeSam" and he would come over and give me a scratch before going back to whatever he was doing. Sometimes Rick's Dad and Cindy's Dad would be together like this for hours, and even though they didn't always talk much I could tell that they liked each other real well; dogs can sense those things.

During these visits it was always a good idea to hang around near the house, because a lot of baking would go on, and that always meant something good to eat. Us dogs weren't allowed in the kitchen during the baking (it got a little crowded in there, with Cindy's Mom and Rick's Mom and Cindy and Rick stopping in every so often to "check on the cookies," so we would kind of hang around on the porch and look hungry. Keltri, who now lived really close by, would sometimes be there too, and we would of course share whatever we had with her.

The house had lots of rooms, so there was plenty of space for all these people, even all at once, and after I would go from room to room, or out on the porch, and always find someone to play with or just be near.

Other people came to visit, too. Rick and Cindy had lots of friends, and they were always coming to stay for the weekend, or for dinner. They all really liked us, and some of them even had their own dogs, who would sometimes come too. Once everyone came at the same time, and that was really fun, because no one got tired of me hounding them for a little back scratch.

But no matter how fun it was with all the visitors, there was something special in the air when Rick and Cindy were together. Sometimes they would sit in front of the fireplace and talk long into the night, the fire burning down to ashes, and other times they would just be together for a long time without saying anything. I always felt so good when they were there, so relaxed and peaceful. There was something of Rick in Cindy, and something of Cindy in Rick. I know that sounds a little strange for a dog to know, but we sometimes just sense things, and I wouldn't even have to be in the same room as them or see them to know that they were with each other.

Every day was like the day before, only better. In the morning, Cindy and Rick would come down to the kitchen and would make breakfast together, and in the summer they would eat outside on the porch, and me and Iris would wait in the corner for them to finish, because there was usually something left over for us, and we always went on a walk together after. Sometimes Rick would go out and bring Cindy back some wildflowers, red, and yellow, and white ones. I didn't know much about flowers but Cindy really loved them, and she and Rick would spend hours in the garden, clearing the ground and planting, and every so often they would stop work and just look at one another and smile.

Once in the spring when we were walking we came to a very green patch of grass with lots of flowers, and it was odd because it was too early in the year for it to be so green. Cindy and Rick decided to build a small bench there, with a little cover, like an arbor, and they would sit there and watch the sun set and the stars come out. We would sit by them there, for it had the same warm feeling as home, and sometimes there Rick would call Cindy Luthien, and she would call him Beren, and they would hold each other and I could hear the sound of their heartbeats as the warm breeze stirred the grass.

* * *

I have been with Cindy and Rick for many dog years, and I bet I am the happiest dog in the world (well, next to Iris and Roy). If I could talk, I'd tell them how glad I am to be part of this family, and how good it feels to be in such a warm and comfortable home.

But I think they know. Dogs can sense those things.

Some Final Thoughts

God summoned the beast from the fields and He said, "Behold people created in my image. Therefore, adore them. You shall protect them in the wilderness, shepherd their flocks, watch over their children, accompany them wherever they may go — even into civilization. You shall be a companion, an ally, a slave.

"To do these things," God said, "I endow you with instincts uncommon to other beasts: faithfulness, devotion and understanding surpassing that of people. Lest it impair your courage, you shall never foresee your death. Lest it impair your loyalty, you shall be blind to the faults of people. Lest it impair your understanding, you are denied the power of words. Let no fault of language cleave an accord beyond that of people with any other beasts — or even people with other people.

"Walk by their sides; sleep in their doorways; forage for them; ward off their enemies; carry their burdens; share their afflictions; love them and comfort them. And in return for this, people will fulfill your needs and wants — which shall be only food, shelter and affection.

"So be silent, and be a friend to people. Guide them along the way to this land that I have promised them. This shall be your destiny and your immortality." So spoke the Lord.

And the dog heard and was content.

— Donald B. Thorburn, *Newsletter of the American Dog Owner's Association, June/July 1996*

In Memory

of

Brian Paul Dale

October 23, 1957 – September 11, 2001

who learned and lived all of these lessons

Bibliography
and Suggested Reading

Blout, Roy (text) and Valerie Shaff (photographer). *If Only You Knew How Much I Smell You.* New York, Little, Brown and Company, Inc., 1998.

Buscalgia, Leo. *Living, Loving and Learning.* New York: Fawcett Columbine, 1982.

Carroll, Lewis. *Through the Looking Glass.* New York: New American Library, 2000.

Donaldson, Jean. *The Culture Clash.* Berkeley, California: James & Kenneth Publishers, 1996.

Gardner, John. *Self Renewal: The Individual and Innovative Society.* W.W. Norton and Company, 1995.

Hoff, Benjamin. *The Tao of Pooh*. New York: Penquin Books, 1982.

Holland, Virgil. *Herding Dogs: Progressive Training*. New York: Howell Book House, 1994.

Kingsolver, Barbara. *Animal Dreams*. New York: Harper Perrennial, 1991.

McCaig, Donald. *Eminent Dogs, Dangerous Men*. New York, The Lyons Press, 1991.

———. *Nop's Hope*. New York: The Lyons Press, 1994.

Masson, Jeffrey Moussaieff. *Dogs Never Lie About Love*. New York: Crown Publishers, 1997.

Pirsig, Robert M. *Zen and the Art of Motorcycle Maintenance*. New York: Bantam Books, 1980.

Sills, Judith. *Excess Baggage*. New York: Penquin Books, 1993.

Vessey-Fitzgerald, Brian. *Animal Anthology*. London: Newnes, 1965.

W.R. Pursche lives in Orlean, Virginia with a dog, two rescued orphan horses, and a somewhat feral cat. He splits his time between writing, teaching, providing business advice, and doing whatever he can to help save and care for dogs and other animals. You can reach him at WRP@lessonstoliveby.com.

If you would like to purchase additional copies, or want to find out how you can raise funds for your local humane organization by buying or selling copies of *Lessons to Live By: The Canine Commandments*, please visit lessonstoliveby.com.

100% of the net proceeds of this edition will be donated to the care and saving of dogs and other animals.

* * *

Printed in the United States
131311LV00001B/547-615/A